TO

DANIEL

ADELANTE
AMIGO
ADELANTE !

5.11.07

THE
MAGIC
MEGAPHONE

Nick Montoya

with

Roger S. Peterson

THE
MAGIC
MEGAPHONE

Nick Montoya

with

Roger S. Peterson

Megaphone Publishing Company
Granite Bay, California

Megaphone Publishing Company, a division of
Megaphone Communications
Granite Bay, California

Megaphone Communications
6873 Douglas Blvd. #121
Granite Bay, California 95746

ISBN: 0-9786304-0-8
ISBN13: 978-0-978630409
Library of Congress Control Number: 2006931806
1. business leadership and management

Cover, book design concepts by Jannetje Anita Thomas of Binding Plus
Illustrations by Dan Bessie ©Binding Plus
Images © JUPITERIMAGES

The Magic Megaphone is a registered trademark of Megaphone Communications, and the following are hereby claimed trademarks used in
commerce by Megaphone Communications: MegaMission, MegaBenefits,
MegaTargets, MegaMagic, MegaPlan, MegaSuccesses and Megaphoners.

"The Magic Megaphone, as the authors and the title state, is a process that
takes less than 60 minutes. However, team leader styles and experience may
differ. Some project leaders may finish a Magic Megaphone session in less
then sixty minutes, and some project leaders may encounter problems that
extend the session a few minutes longer. Nonetheless, sixty minutes
should be your goal."

Printed in the United States of America

Dedicated To

John Whiteside
a long-time friend, mentor,
coach and the inspiration for
The Magic Megaphone

TABLE OF CONTENTS

Foreword 9

Introduction 10

PART ONE · The Magic Steps 17

Step 0 — Re-Orient 19

Step 1 — MegaMission 29

Step 2 — MegaBenefits 43

Step 3 — MegaTargets 53

Step 4 — MegaMagic 67

Step 5 — MegaPlan 77

PART TWO · MegaSuccesses 103

MegaSuccesses 105

MegaQuestions 107

MegaThanks 121

The Magic Megaphone®

MAGIC MEGAPHONE
A quick, simple management tool that works in any organization

Most managers and project leaders assemble a personal toolbox of techniques and processes that work well for them. They use these tools to solve problems, attack special situations, and manage people and projects.

As more project teams and managers, both inside and outside of Intel, have used the Magic Megaphone, word has spread about its speed and simplicity. It has become a reliable tool because it works for so many applications.

Teams are using the Magic Megaphone, not just to get projects out of a rut, but also to spark innovation, to manage transitions, to develop marketing and communication plans, and to assist in team building. Just as important, teams learn the Magic Megaphone is a great first step in project planning because the technique delivers results faster than more complicated processes.

I've noticed something else about the Magic Megaphone: Project teams actually have fun using it. This process changes their thinking about the art of the possible and takes less than an hour to complete. In a very real sense, the Magic Megaphone replaces project team frustration with project team rejuvenation. For global companies running across 24 time zones, that's important.

This will become one of the most widely used management tools ever developed.

John Johnson
Vice-President and Chief Information Officer
Intel Corporation

STUCK?

FEELING STUCK? Of course you are. That's why you picked up this book. And now you want to know how it's going to help you . . .

During my twenty-five years at Intel, I conducted more than 200 Magic Megaphone sessions with colleagues. I've also shared the process with many other businesses and organizations. It's been well-tested with tough audiences and the beneficial results reported back are consistent:

- It's a proven method for aligning team members and getting everyone on the same page. Project teams quickly reach consensus on their core mission and message.

- Project members start to see who the real customer or target is and why targeting a plan is essential.

- Team members become motivated and inspired when they are allowed to state the most ideal reactions they want their target audiences to have toward project accomplishments.

- It works – like magic. It's simple, effective, and produces the desired results and sounds of success.

Nick Montoya

About those ants on the cover. Ants are industrious and untiring. We have watched them carry twice their weight as they communicate down the line. These hard working critters have often prompted us to say "WOW!" But ours are a special breed of ants – Megaphoner ants. They are going to help you become magical in Step 4 of the Magic Megaphone process. Watch for them.

LET'S GET UNSTUCK. OK. You're feeling stuck. So, what can you do about it?

RECOGNIZE IT – Do these sound familiar?

"I can't seem to get management to pay attention. I can't even get them in the room."

"My meeting attendance is sparse. The project team members request too many reschedules. Latecomers delay meetings."

"Our problem statement isn't well-defined. Team members just can't agree on how to define the problem."

"My team members aren't in sync. Infighting and turf issues are getting us stuck. Geez, it's frustrating, and the deadline isn't waiting, either."

"We can't agree on who our target audience is."

"We have no communication plan. Heck, we can't even agree on a project plan!"

"Oh, we have a mission statement. But it's soooo long and soooo sugary. How can anyone follow it?"

"My team members are frustrated and stressed by the sluggishness of the project. We're missing all the deadlines."

"I have one negative person on my project team. Every new idea we suggest gets shot down. But we can't remove that person."

"I was assigned a project, assembled a team, and we were getting up to speed – then we discovered the funding wasn't adequate."

"Hidden agendas are rampant on this project team."

IF THESE SOUND WAY TOO FAMILIAR, THIS BOOK IS FOR YOU.

ADMIT IT

You are in the middle of a stalled, lifeless, 'going nowhere' project. It is keeping you awake at night. You keep asking yourself . . .

What did we do wrong?

How am I going to get this project back on track?

FACE IT

Being stuck is commonplace in business. It is frustrating when managers or colleagues do not react enthusiastically to your initiatives, events, campaigns, or other projects. When their response is not what you hoped for, how do you react? Disappointed, right?

SOLVE IT . . . within 60 minutes

Solve it, in 60 minutes, using a quick and easy management tool called The Magic Megaphone. The Magic Megaphone process will help you pull your team together on your project's purpose, the most desirable results, the most important target audience – and help you outline a simple two-page plan that will be the most productive daily reminder you ever displayed in your workspace.

YOU DO HAVE ALTERNATIVES

Many seminars, courses, and books are far more comprehensive than *The Magic Megaphone*, complete with diagrams, flow charts, and software. They are probably all effective if you put sufficient time into learning the systems. You can also hire a management consultant if you have the budget.

Courses, consultants
your time, your money
your choice . . .

But if you're stuck right now, you need to get unstuck right now. And *The Magic Megaphone* helps you get your project back on track within 60 minutes.

HOW THE MAGIC MEGAPHONE WORKS

Compared to more elaborate project management tools, *The Magic Megaphone* can help you:

- Rethink your approach to project management
- Break through barriers that get your team stuck
- Identify a short statement of purpose that people can actually remember
- Translate your purpose into obvious benefits
- Identify the right audiences who will want those benefits
- Articulate the most ideal outcome for the project
- Define an action plan for your audiences
- Generate the reactions you really want to hear

THE MEGAPHONE ANALOGY. *For centuries, speakers and leaders have used megaphones to amplify their voice above the ambient noise. The audience listened and got the message.*

LIFE WAS SIMPLER THEN

But in today's global e-marketplace, managers and project leaders compete for a decreasing share of a precious commodity: attention span. Attention span is especially important because most employees work on many different projects all at the same time.

Most work we all do is project based. Projects are approved because managers who approve projects anticipate some added value from the project.

These modern realities all require a little Magic.

Part One

The Magic Steps

Putting the Magic Megaphone

to work for you and your team . . .

in less than 60 minutes

RE-ORIENT

how you look at
projects and
problems

TO GET UNSTUCK, YOU MUST FIRST
unlearn. To unlearn, you must re-orient your thinking.
Since we are all creatures of habit, we sometimes have
to unlearn old things before we can learn new things.
Habits become so ingrained, we forget to re-examine
them to see if they are still working for us instead of
against us.

Let's get some unlearning out of the way. By learning the
following three simple Magic Megaphone Principles,
you will be assisted in unlearning and breaking habits
that hold you back from getting unstuck.

REORIENTATION #1

SIMPLE IS BETTER

Yes, that's what we mean. A simple way that works
quickly is surely better than a complex method that
allows the project to remain stuck.

The Magic Megaphone is probably the simplest management tool you will ever use. We're not against all the

tools developed by consultants and universities. We're not saying you should throw out elaborate planning and forecasting systems. Yet, you can get stuck in them. The Magic Megaphone is simpler and faster. So why not use it first?

REORIENTATION #2

85% IS OK

Many teams get stuck in the planning stages of projects by trying to be perfectionists. They strive for 100% completeness and perfection in everything they do. They spend days working on "wordsmithing" mission statements or analyzing every single plan detail.

But all that keeps teams from getting started. The Magic Megaphone gives you and your team permission to be just 85% complete. If that sounds somehow incomplete and unfinished, consider this: It's far more important to have a plan at the 85% level that gets a team into action producing results immediately, than it is to have a 100% plan that never makes it out of the conference room. 85% surely includes the key things anyhow, so get started on those key things rather than being stuck searching for the remaining – and minor – 15%.

REORIENTATION #3

THINK "WOW!"

Many corporate cultures ask us to think so analytically we end up with all the reasons an idea will not work. How many times do ideas fizzle that way? Too often, this thinking becomes the reason we get stuck in the first place. Analytical thinking has its place. We, the authors, love analysis. But it can drag on and on and get a team stuck too.

SO START THINKING that way. Think WOW! as you complete each Magic Megaphone step.

WOW! There's a good reason our project exists. It's great to be a part of something that's a big deal to this company.

WOW! The benefits we provide are awesome and exciting. They have "value-added" written all over them.

WOW! Our targets have faces and names. We will make them proud.

WOW! So, this is what success sounds like. This is entirely possible.

MOVING ON!

Consider these three simple principles as the Magic Dust required to get your project back on track.

Magic Megaphone
Principles

1. SIMPLE IS BETTER
2. 85% IS OK
3. THINK "WOW!"

YOU ARE ABOUT TO BECOME A MEGAPHONER

We'll get right into it as we help you get unstuck with the problem or project that came to mind when you first saw this book.

We'll walk you through the tool that will get you unstuck and help you better manage your project . . . using the Magic Megaphone.

You are about to become a Megaphoner. In the back of the book you will find a Magic Megaphone template that you can tear out.

Tear it out now. (*If you need more, just visit us at www.magicmegaphone.com.*)

MEET YOUR FELLOW MEGAPHONERS

The following stories are based on actual projects and those project teams were really stuck. As you are learning the Magic Megaphone process, you will watch as your four colleagues do the same. Think of them as fellow Megaphoners, as if you were all on a Magic Megaphone discussion board.

Introducing the Megaphoners

MEET CARLOS

Hello,

I'm Carlos. I'm 32 years old and a senior project leader at my company. I was recently assigned the task of leading the merger of two engineering teams into one. This merger will support manufacturing with one consolidated information technology team. The first few meetings with my project team did not go well. We had a difficult time agreeing on a consolidated mission statement (and I don't think everyone has really bought in yet). In addition, turf issues involving the old organizations keep rising to the surface. Management is breathing down my neck to get this consolidation underway and you could definitely say I'm feeling stuck right now.

MEET PHYLLIS

Hi. I'm Phyllis.

I'm 35 years old and went back to school and received my business degree with an emphasis in finance. I've been a finance analyst for the past two years. I volunteered for a task force responsible for defining and implementing an employee recognition system for finance employees worldwide. Right before our first meeting, the task force leader had to step down. I volunteered to take his place and lead this team. I didn't have a lot of prior project management experience, but I thought I could handle it. I wanted to show my managers that I was capable of jobs beyond a finance analyst. After two meetings, it became clear that I was not going to get the support of the other team members. I learned others wanted the leadership role and were now resentful and difficult to work with. Talk about being stuck . . . I'm definitely there.

MEET JOHN

I'm John and I'm a dentist.

I've had my own practice for the past fifteen years. My employee turnover is below industry average and my patient base is established and very loyal.

My children will be entering college in the next few years. I feel that my practice is stagnant and I don't have a solid plan to take it to higher levels. Since my employees have been with me a long time, I'm concerned that their productivity may be on the low side. I need to spend more time with my kids, but know that I need to grow the business in order to secure their future and provide long-term employment for my employees. I just don't have the time or energy to focus on the longer term business plan. I've been feeling stuck for a while now.

MEET SADHANA

Hello.

I'm Sadhana, age 29, and a software engineer at a hi-tech firm. I've been in the same position for seven years. I'm feeling burnt out and know that my productivity and performance are suffering. I would love to work in marketing. I've made it my personal project to get a job in our company's marketing department. I've always had an interest in marketing and, before college, I helped our family business with many marketing ideas and plans. I've talked to a couple of the marketing managers and they have discouraged me from applying for open positions because I do not have a formal education in business or marketing. I am feeling stuck and burnt out!

With support from fellow Megaphoners, you won't stress as much over your project . . . especially if we can help you get it unstuck in less than 60 minutes. In fact, you may begin to have some fun. As you begin to get your project back on track, we remind you that the Magic Megaphone Principles will play an important role.

YOUR TURN

It's time to identify the project you want to work on.

• Which project is stuck?

• Which project is not progressing and is falling short of expectations? (*More than likely it's the project that first came to mind when you saw the title of this book*).

Write the name of your project on the top of the tear-out sheet, or write it here.

_____

By the way, here's what your fellow Megaphoners wrote on the top of their sheets:

Carlos: IT Manufacturing Engineering Consolidation

Phyllis: Finance Employee Recognition Task Force

John: Grow Dental Practice

Sadhana: Get a Marketing Job

Keep your eyes open for the Sync Up Time sections that will regularly appear. We will check in on Carlos, Phyllis, John, and Sadhana to see how they are doing.

MegaMission

?

why does
your project
exist?

MEGAMISSION™ DOES NOT MEAN *mission
statement*. Mission statements rarely work.

Many project teams become deeply stuck at this beginning
stage. Or, just as bad, the team skips this step altogether.

A project team can spend mind numbing hours debating
the wording of a mission statement that will rarely be read
again. Most mission statements are difficult to remember.
They put you to sleep with bloated sentences and preten-
tious words. But an easier and simpler alternative exists
that gets you unstuck fast: your MegaMission.

> YOUR MEGAMISSION SHOULD BE SIMPLE, direct,
> and memorable. It should not sound as lofty as the
> United Nations Charter.

> THE MEGAMISSION CONCEPT IS FLEXIBLE. It can be
> a general goal or a precise objective, or it can be a
> simple statement of purpose.

A MegaMission should be obvious — a simple statement or phrase that addresses the reason for the project's existence. Just ask, "Why are we here? What is this project really about?" If the team has not asked those basic questions, no endless mission statement will ever get you unstuck.

SIMPLE IS BETTER

We are not talking about 100% completeness either. That is what inflated missions statements try to do. Instead, just capture 85% (Magic Megaphone Principle #2) of the project's essential driving purpose and get the entire project team aligned around that in minutes. That last 15% will waste hours of time that should be used to push your team into action.

85% IS OK

The decision is yours. It is your project and your choice. But so is the accountability. So why not choose something that is quick, easy . . . and gets you unstuck? Let's get back to the project you chose to work on. Ask yourself something many project teams never ask:

WHY DOES THIS PROJECT EXIST?

What's your team or task force here to do? Consider how many times you've participated in projects that went off course. A likely culprit: assumption. Too often we start a project assuming it is obvious what the project is all about. Then later you hear colleagues or managers outside the project team say, "Gee, this is not what I thought this project was all about. I thought we were focused on X, not Y?"

Reality: The project or problem statement may not have been clear from the start.

SYNC UP TIME

Your fellow Megaphoners just completed Step 1, the Mega-Mission. How did they do? Here's what they had to say:

31

To: Megaphoners
Fm: Carlos
Re: MegaMission

Project: IT Manufacturing Engineering Consolidation

After discussing the Magic Megaphone principles, the team quickly realized that we had spent too much time creating a long-winded mission statement that several of us weren't enthusiasic about. This is how it read:

"IT Manufacturing Engineering Consolidation's mission is to consolidate the information technology teams in order to achieve economies of scale, leverage on the best known methods of operation, and reduce cost to best support Manufacturing's IT needs."

I asked the team to state simply the core reason this new merged organization should exist and what is it that we are really after. It took only a couple minutes before someone said, "To be the best manufacturing computing support organization in the world." I looked around. All were nodding with a look on their faces like, "Yup, that's it!" Oddly enough, it was the first galvanizing moment this new project team had experienced.

I was thinking, "Yeah! There is light at the end of this tunnel."

Carlos

To: MEGAPHONERS
FM: PHYLLIS
RE: MEGAMISSION

PROJECT: FINANCE EMPLOYEE RECOGNITION TASK FORCE

Hi Everyone,

During our next meeting, I introduced the Magic Mega-phone process and immediately asked the team why this team existed in the first place. I told them that we did not have to be 100% complete; if we were at the 85% level, that would be fine. Giving my team (and me) permission to be less than complete seemed to open up conversation, even from two colleagues who seemed most resentful towards me. In fact, one of them piped up and said enthusiastically, "It's simple – we exist to recognize employees for a job well done." Everyone was agreeing. I said, "If everyone agrees, then that's our MegaMission." That took less than five minutes. I could see that the team members were ready to go on to the next step. Phew!

Phyllis

To: Megaphoners
Fm: John
Re: MegaMission

PROJECT: GROW DENTAL PRACTICE

Hello Megaphoners:

I always wondered if I needed a mission statement for my practice, but never got around to it. Honestly, I didn't see the value. Most of the mission statements I had seen in other businesses seemed to be ignored. I needed to approach it more effectively. Otherwise, why bother? I got into the Magic Megaphone and asked myself, "What is it that I am really trying to accomplish?" In a matter of a few minutes, the answer came to me: I need to grow my revenue 50% in three years. "50 in 3" is truly my MegaMission. I found myself actually excited about the future instead of feeling stressed out.

John

To: MEGAPHONERS
FM: SADHANA
RE: MEGAMISSION

PROJECT: GET A MARKETING JOB

Since my project was more of a personal project or goal, I wasn't sure that the Magic Megaphone tool could help me. But I needed help fast, so I decided it was worth a try. The MegaMission was really simple for me. What I was after ended up being what my personal project was all about: Get a Marketing Job! It doesn't get any more basic that that, and it's to-the-point. Seeing my MegaMission on the chart makes me want it even more. This process is making me feel focused and revitalized.

Sadhana

YOUR TURN

What is the MegaMission for your project? Remember to apply the Magic Megaphone Principles.

Magic Megaphone
Principles

1. SIMPLE IS BETTER
2. 85% IS OK
3. THINK "WOW!"

Answer this question:

WHAT IS THE REASON FOR YOUR PROJECT'S EXISTENCE?

Now write down why your project was started and why it exists.

_____

_____

_____

_____

_____

_____

Write it in ten words or less.

_____

_____

_____

Yes, YOU CAN DO IT

Now transcribe this on your Magic Megaphone tear-out template.

MAGIC MEGAPHONES IN PROGRESS

The following pages show how your fellow Megaphoners' Megaphones are looking after Step 1. Make sure your Megaphone template is filled out in the same manner.

CARLOS

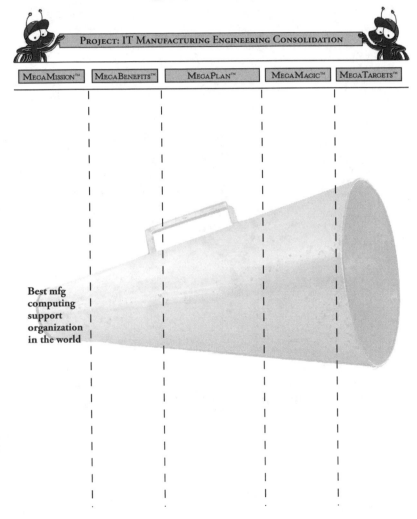

PROJECT: IT MANUFACTURING ENGINEERING CONSOLIDATION

| MegaMission™ | MegaBenefits™ | MegaPlan™ | MegaMagic™ | MegaTargets™ |

Best mfg
computing
support
organization
in the world

PHYLLIS

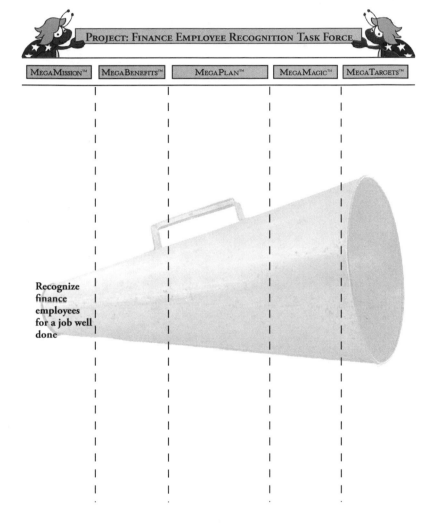

PROJECT: FINANCE EMPLOYEE RECOGNITION TASK FORCE

MegaMission™	MegaBenefits™	MegaPlan™	MegaMagic™	MegaTargets™

Recognize
finance
employees
for a job well
done

JOHN

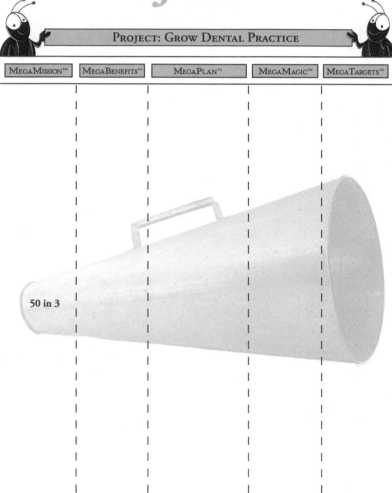

PROJECT: GROW DENTAL PRACTICE

| MegaMission™ | MegaBenefits™ | MegaPlan™ | MegaMagic™ | MegaTargets™ |

50 in 3

SADHANA

PROJECT: GET A MARKETING JOB

| MegaMission™ | MegaBenefits™ | MegaPlan™ | MegaMagic™ | MegaTargets™ |

Get a
marketing
job

YOU ARE NOW FINISHED WITH STEP 1

Time to move on to Step 2 where we will help you translate
your MegaMission into key benefits.

MegaBenefits

translating your
MegaMission into
key values and benefits

MISSION STATEMENTS HAVE ANOTHER
problem. Once project members agree on the wording, they
often lean back, saying, "Hey, we finally got that finished.
We're in good shape now." Wrong. The job is not done. It
has barely started.

> *Mission statements that are not translated
> into desired values and benefits are powerless
> words.*

That is why most mission statements never become more
than fancy signs in the company lobbies. The authors know
your lobby sign is a masterpiece of commercial art. But
when was the last time you saw anyone actually stop to read
it in the morning?

In Step 2 you will translate your MegaMission into simply
stated values and benefits – your MegaBenefits.™

MEGABENEFITS BECOME the talking points of what you are trying to accomplish and what your project is all about.

MegaBenefits unite your project team members around a rationale for action: what the project's value is to them and to the entire company.

Do not fall into that old rut of trying to produce a 100% complete and perfect list of values and benefits. Perfect results are rare. Just strive for 85% completeness – the most obvious and significant values and benefits. Think of Mega-Benefits as the engines behind your MegaMission.

Consider your chosen project and ask yourself . . .

What are the key benefits that are reflective of my MegaMission?

What difference will this project make when it is completed?

How will my company, organization, or department benefit when this project succeeds?

Regardless of how many people you are trying to reach with your MegaMission, the key values and benefits of that mission – your MegaBenefits – remain constant. They are your foundation.

SIMPLE IS BETTER

Reduce your benefit statements to short bullets. Acronyms are acceptable, as long as your project team knows what they mean.

85% IS OK

Do some creative thinking—brainstorming—about benefits. Allow everyone to contribute. Your list does not need to be 100% perfect and complete, because delivering 85% of the possible benefits would be quite an accomplishment. When you think you are finished with the brainstorming, add an ellipsis (… or dot.dot.dot) in the MegaBenefits section of your Magic Megaphone to show you worked out the list to the 85% level.

THINK WOW!

If you are feeling stuck, it's because you really care about your project and the benefits it will provide. Try this. As you brainstorm, think "WOW!" Choose the benefits with the most WOW! power. If you were successful delivering those benefits, the reactions would be quite positive, right? So get into the WOW! mood now, because that mood will come up again in the step called MegaMagic.

SYNC UP TIME

Your fellow Megaphoners have just completed Step 2, MegaBenefits. Time to check in with them and see how they did.

To: MEGAPHONERS

FM: CARLOS

RE: MEGABENEFITS

PROJECT: IT MANUFACTURING ENGINEERING CONSOLIDATION

Our team started out by discussing how our department would benefit. We quickly realized that it was more important to focus on how the company will benefit. The brainstorming took a completely different turn. The Think WOW! principle seemed to energize the team, and the momentum from the MegaMission task increased.

Here are the MegaBenefits we came up with:

- Increases volume and reduces TPT (throughput time)
- Sets up manufacturing as a competitive advantage
- Makes IT proactive vs. reactive
- Quality increases
- Reduces TCO (total cost of ownership)
- Increases IT value to the company
- …

WOW! Then it hit us – we now had the key talking points for an upcoming presentation to management. It felt good that we were looking at this from the bigger picture. So far, during the Magic Megaphone process, turf issues have not arisen. What a change for all to be on the same page.

Carlos

To: Megaphoners

Fm: Phyllis

Re: MegaBenefits

Project: Finance Employee Recognition Task Force

Hi again,

Our team did not have any problem coming up with the MegaBenefits associated with our MegaMission. We completed this step in about 10 minutes! Each of the five team members contributed. In a way, the Magic Megaphone is turning out to be a great tool for teambuilding. Oh, here are our MegaBenefits:

- Employee satisfaction
- Performance linked to group objectives
- Fosters great workplace value
- Provides consistency with other departments
- Engagement and retention of employees
- ...

Talk to you later. Bye.

Phyllis

47

To: Megaphoners
Fm: John
Re: MegaBenefits

Project: Grow Dental Practice

This step had a big impact on me. By actually writing down the benefits of accomplishing 50% revenue growth in 3 years, I felt the fog start to clear. I inherently knew the benefits, but just writing them out made them seem more reachable. I've been into this only a few minutes, and I feel more energetic about my practice than I have been in a very long time. I'm ready to do the work necessary to see these benefits come to fruition.

Here are my MegaBenefits:

- Financial security
- No-worry college funding
- Greater disposable income
- More efficiency
- Growth opportunities for employees
- More opportunities to give back to the community
- ...

John

To: MEGAPHONERS
FM: SADHANA
RE: MEGABENEFITS

PROJECT: GET A MARKETING JOB

Hello fellow Megaphoners,

It took me a few minutes to get started on this. My engineering background took over and I was trying to be exact about it. I finally remembered that it is OK to be at an 85% level of completeness. After that, it came easy. When I get my marketing job, here is how the company, my family, and I will benefit:

- Company retains a good employee
- Match passion with job
- Utilize software engineering experience in marketing
- Less stress
- Increased productivity
- …

I liked coming up with these because I am now able to state what benefits I'm after. I wish I would have done this before I met with those two marketing managers.

Sadhana

YOUR TURN

Translate your MegaMission into MegaBenefits. For now, just brainstorm some key benefits.

Avoid sentences – use bullet points instead. Remember to apply the Magic Megaphone Principles.

_____

_____

_____

_____

_____

_____

_____

Summary of the key points regarding MegaBenefits

- Keep it at 85% completeness
- Think of benefits to the overall company
- Do it as a team; don't impose it from the top down
- Your MegaBenefits are constant; they do not change unless circumstances change

MAGIC MEGAPHONE in progress:

We will follow Phyllis's Magic Megaphone in progress. Here is how it looks after Step 2:

PHYLLIS

PROJECT: FINANCE EMPLOYEE RECOGNITION TASK FORCE

MegaMission™	MegaBenefits™	MegaPlan™	MegaMagic™	MegaTargets™

Recognize employees for a job well done

- Employee satisfaction
- Link performance to group objectives
- Fosters great workplace value
- Provides consistency with other departments
- Engagement and retention of employees
- ...

Now update your own Magic Megaphone template

You are finished with Step 2. Now we proceed to Step 3 where you will identify the key individuals and groups you want to target for this project. These targets will play an important role in your success.

51

MEGATARGETS

who cares
or who
should care

IN STEP 2, YOU TRANSLATED YOUR Mega-Mission into words and values your team can understand: MegaBenefits. The next step is to identify who cares – or who should care – about your project: your MegaTargets.™

We are typically too casual about who is interested in or affected by project goals. If your team has not carefully discussed affected targets and specifically identified them, your project might become stuck – if you are not already stuck. Step 3 helps you attach names and faces to your goals, making the task far less abstract.

WHO IS IMPORTANT TO YOUR PROJECT'S SUCCESS?

If you can identify who is important to your success, your project is more likely to succeed. Examples of who cares or who should care about your project include employees, managers, senior executives, project team members, partners, stakeholders, beneficiaries, and those who allocate vital resources to your project. A target could also be external, commercial customers.

THINK CREATIVELY about the "who." Not all influential people in organizations are executives and managers.

Many non-managers are respected for their intelligent analysis. Other influential colleagues may be subtle coalition builders, working behind the scenes during changes or crises. Some are magnets for employee attention because of their wit . . . or their sarcasm. These folks can be your ambassadors, speaking up for your project in meetings. Do not overlook such key influencers.

Take some time to brainstorm with your team. Identify who cares about your project and who should care about your project. It is important to use specific names as much as possible for all MegaTargets. Your team may develop a long list of names. However, given limited time and resources for your project, you will eventually have to rank the names in order of importance so you can identify and concentrate on the top MegaTarget.

who cares and who should care these are your MegaTargets

SYNC UP TIME

We should now see how your fellow Megaphoners did with applying Step 3 to their respective projects.

To: Megaphoners

Fm: Carlos

Re: MegaTargets

Project: IT Manufacturing Engineering Consolidation

I took extra care in setting up this particular step for the team, because I feared old turf issues could arise. I knew that team members were very opinionated about the "who" related to this project.

I followed the instructions and asked the team to brainstorm a list of individuals and key organizations who care or who should care about the success of our project. I asked them to be specific and assured them there are no wrong answers in brainstorming. Each one of us would have a turn at providing a name.

It worked. We came up with the following list in a matter of minutes:

- Manufacturing management team: Bob, GW, EH Tan, Pat, Jason
- CIO and her direct staff
- Michael (our boss)
- All IT employees
- All manufacturing employees (users)
- IT Manufacturing mgt team

Probably more names could have been added, but we concluded the list was just fine at the 85% level.

Carlos

To: Megaphoners

Fm: Phyllis

Re: MegaTargets

Project: Finance Employee Recognition Task Force

Hi team,

Members of our task force had never before been asked to identify key targets, nor had they ever been asked the question "who cares or should care" about the success of the project. Many observed this was really critical to any project's success. Just asking it excited the whole team! Here's how our brainstorm ended up:

- All Finance employees
- CFO
- HR manager that supports Finance
- Bob (Finance mgr sponsoring this project)
- Judy P. (On Finance staff – key influencer)
- Country managers: SH, TE and GG
- Tanya (administrative team leader)
- Barry (my manager and peer to Bob)

Several people showed up on the list whom I would not have considered. Everyone seemed to be on the same page. So far, so good.

Phyllis

To: Megaphoners

Fm: John

Re: MegaTargets

PROJECT: GROW DENTAL PRACTICE

Having just written my MegaMission and MegaBenefits, coming up with MegaTargets was an easy task. Here they are:

- My family
- My staff
- Current patients
- New patients
- My vendors
- Community organizations I volunteer at
- Dental associations I belong to

John

To: Megaphoners
Fm: Sadhana
Re: MegaTargets

PROJECT: GET A MARKETING JOB

Hello fellow Megaphoners,

This step was eye-opening. I realized that a lot of different people have a key stake in my success at work. I was thinking too narrowly before.

My MegaTargets:

- Phillip (my current boss)
- Kristen (my HR rep)
- RL, AM and JB (key marketing managers)
- Rav (my fiancé)
- My family (Mother & Father)
- John W. (my boss's boss)
- Faye (a friend of mine in marketing who is highly regarded and influential)

I also realized that some individuals were missing from my list, such as a marketing mentor or a career counselor. I heard of people in my department who had taken advantage of company mentor and career counseling programs. This step woke me up to the fact that people are out there who can help me. I don't have to attack this all by myself.

Sadhana

YOUR TURN

Who are your MegaTargets?

Who cares about your project? Who should care? Who has a stake in your project's success? Who will benefit from it? Who allocates the resources for your project? Who may be doubtful about your project's worth? Who is not listening? Who can help you win over support from others?

Brainstorm names and add them below, but also transcribe them onto your Megaphone tear-out template.

- _____
- _____
- _____
- _____
- _____
- _____
- _____
- _____
- _____

Now that you have listed names of people who care or should care about your project, it is time to select one of them.

The criteria for selecting your main MegaTarget can vary. You can choose the target who is most important to your success or choose the one who will be most influential in helping you get unstuck. Or you can choose the manager who holds the purse strings.

MANY MEGAPHONERS have fun selecting the main MegaTarget. They give team members two or three votes each (first choice, second choice, third choice).

Team members then place their rankings next to the two or three people most important to the project's success. The one target with the most votes becomes the main MegaTarget.

Whom did your fellow Megaphoners select as their principal MegaTarget?

Carlos's MegaTarget Selection
IT MANUFACTURING ENGINEERING CONSOLIDATION

"This was an easy conversation for us. Our key stakeholder is the IT Manufacturing management team. If the team does not buy into our plan, we will not be able to proceed much further."

- Manufacturing management team: Bob, GW, EH Tan, Pat, Jason
- CIO and her direct staff
- Michael (our boss)
- All IT employees
- All manufacturing employees (users)
- IT Manufacturing mgt team

Phyllis's MegaTarget Selection
FINANCE EMPLOYEE RECOGNITION TASK FORCE

"My team liked the idea of voting to select the most important target. Each team member had three votes. If they felt strongly enough about one of the targets, they could place all three of their votes on that particular one. As it turned out, "All Finance Employees" received the most votes. That made sense, as they are the real customers for this project team."

- All Finance employees
- CFO
- HR manager that supports Finance
- Bob (Finance mgr sponsoring this project)
- Judy P. (On Finance staff – key influencer)
- Country managers: SH, TE and GG
- Tanya (Admin team lead and key partner)
- Barry (my manager and peer to Bob)

John's MegaTarget Selection
GROW DENTAL PRACTICE

"I need to involve my staff. I can't make it happen without them."

- My family
- My staff
- Current patients
- New patients
- My vendors
- Community organizations I volunteer at
- Dental associations I belong to

Sadhana's MegaTarget Selection
GET A MARKETING JOB

"I chose the marketing managers as my main MegaTarget, as I will ultimately work in one of their organizations (positive thinking)."

- Phillip (my current boss)
- Kristen (my HR rep)
- RL, AM and JB (key marketing managers)
- Rav (my fiancé)
- My family (Mother & Father)
- John W. (my boss's boss)
- Faye (a friend of mine in marketing who is highly regarded and influential)

YOUR TURN

Select your main MegaTarget

_____

Circle that person or organization on your tear-out template.

MAGIC MEGAPHONE in progress.

This is how Phyllis's Magic Megaphone looks after she identified her MegaTargets and selected one main MegaTarget.

PHYLLIS

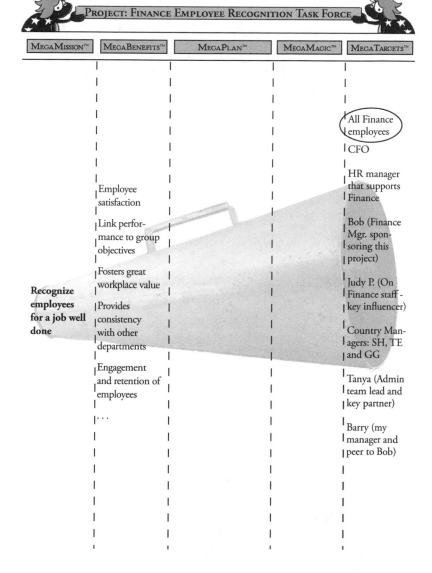

PROJECT: FINANCE EMPLOYEE RECOGNITION TASK FORCE

MEGAMISSION™	MEGABENEFITS™	MEGAPLAN™	MEGAMAGIC™	MEGATARGETS™
Recognize employees for a job well done	Employee satisfaction			All Finance employees
	Link performance to group objectives			CFO
	Fosters great workplace value			HR manager that supports Finance
	Provides consistency with other departments			Bob (Finance Mgr. sponsoring this project)
	Engagement and retention of employees			Judy P. (On Finance staff - key influencer)
	. . .			Country Managers: SH, TE and GG
				Tanya (Admin team lead and key partner)
				Barry (my manager and peer to Bob)

UPDATE YOUR TEMPLATE

Now take your tear-out template and update the MegaTargets portion of your Magic Megaphone. List all the targets you brainstormed on your Megaphone template, but circle the one MegaTarget you and your team decided to focus on.

You might wonder why the column for MegaTargets is on the far right side of the template rather than next to the MegaBenefits column. It's all about using a megaphone to amplify your message. You speak into the small end; the audience hears you from the large end.

Congratulations. You are now finished with Step 3. So far, you've answered three basic questions about your project:

WHAT IS THIS PROJECT REALLY ABOUT? (MegaMission)

WHY IS IT IMPORTANT? (MegaBenefits)

WHO CARES OR SHOULD CARE? (MegaTarget)

IT IS TIME TO CREATE SOME MAGIC.

MegaMagic

what does

success

sound like?

NOW THAT YOU HAVE IDENTIFIED YOUR MegaTarget, it is time for the real magic of the Magic Megaphone.

IMAGINE it is three months from today. Your project came to an end. You have just returned from a meeting with your MegaTarget during which you reported on the project's results. The meeting went extremely well.

But after you leave that meeting, you escape to a secluded spot. You tap yourself three times on the head with a magic wand that instantly turns you into a special Megaphoner ant. Now you can crawl back under the door to your Mega-Target's office and actually listen to what is being said about the success of your project.

What would you really like to hear your MegaTarget say?

67

WHAT WOULD SUCH reactions and praise sound like? Allow yourself to imagine ideal results.

This is the step in the Magic Megaphone that really excites and motivates project teams. You will quickly see it in their faces and hear it in their voices.

Why? Because this step breaks an old habit about defining results: being timid.

STEP 4 IS NOT ABOUT BEING TIMID

But to break the timid habit, you have to think differently about the possibilities.

It is time to think "WOW!"

To really get the most out of Step 4, you have to think of the best possible outcome. The best outcome is that your project is so successful your MegaTarget is almost speechless.

Almost speechless. You want your MegaTarget to be so impressed that he or she says "WOW!" at the beginning of every comment made about your project. That "WOW!" is what we call your MegaMagic.™ So we have one rule in Step 4: Each listing your team makes in the MegaMagic column must start with the word "WOW!"

Do you want to settle for something less enthusiastic? Why bother doing the project for some passive reaction?

INVOLVE THE WHOLE TEAM

Go around the room and ask each team member to contribute one reaction they would love to hear the MegaTarget say. List each statement in quotation marks starting with the word "WOW!"

This is what makes Step 4 a real eye-opener for your team. When you think your list is about 85% complete, you are done.

Did it ever occur to you that you are entitled to have fun with every project?

No, starting each comment with "WOW!" is not silly! We are conditioned to avoid thinking so optimistically. All too often we miss the fun and excitement this kind of thinking brings to project management. Did it ever occur to you that you are entitled to have fun with every project? Until now, you have not had much fun with projects because you have never heard "WOW!" after you finished.

Maybe because you've never started with "WOW!"

SYNC UP TIME

What are your fellow Megaphoners doing? What praises did they list for their MegaTargets?

To: Megaphoners

Fm: Carlos

Re: MegaMagic

Project: IT Manufacturing Engineering Consolidation

"WOW!" Pardon the pun, but what can I say? After this step, every team member now really believes our MegaMission is possible and within reach: We will become the best manufacturing computing organization in the world.

I set this step up by asking the team, *"Imagine it's three months from now and we exceeded all expectations. We just came out of a meeting with our management team and it went great. We left the room, but magically we turned ourselves into ants and crept back into the room so we could hear what they were really saying about our project. In the very best possible light, and starting each comment with a wow, what is it that they are saying?"*

It took a minute for them to get started, but once they did it was as if the floodgates were opened. It was awesome. Here's our MegaMagic:

"WOW! This team not only executed flawlessly, but they provided a vision the entire organization can get behind."

"WOW! I'm inspired. The team deserves our full support."

"WOW! This is a fine example of how IT really adds value to our company."

"WOW! Our manufacturing partners are already experiencing the benefit of the consolidation. I'm getting tons of positive feedback."

"WOW! This team demonstrated leadership and exceeded my expectations."

I hope your Step 4 was as successful as mine. The entire team is feeling pretty good right now.

Later,

Carlos

To: Megaphoners
Fm: Phyllis
Re: MegaMagic

PROJECT: FINANCE EMPLOYEE RECOGNITION TASK FORCE

Finance people are analytical and have a hard time drawing conclusions without hard evidence. I know; I'm one of them. I set up the magic ant scenario as crawling into an employee's office after the employee just received recognition for a job well done. It worked. The team had no problem coming up with "WOWs!" In fact, one team member commented, "Our job is to ensure the MegaMagic happens for our employees. If we do that, we will have succeeded." I couldn't have said it better.

"WOW! That was awesome. My work is really valued and appreciated here."

"WOW! I'm really glad to be a part of this organization."

"WOW! The recognition team did an outstanding job. The best recognition system I have ever experienced."

"WOW! Finance is a great place to work."

"WOW! This means so much to me. I really worked hard on this task and I wasn't sure that management even noticed. Now, I know they do."

Pretty cool, huh?

Bye for now,

Phyllis

To: Megaphoners
Fm: John
Re: MegaMagic

PROJECT: GROW DENTAL PRACTICE

Here's the MegaMagic I will be waiting to hear from my staff:

"WOW! There's a business plan for growth, and I'm part of it."

"WOW! Dr. J is on it. There is definitely renewed energy and excitement in the office. I'm going to be on it, too."

"WOW! I am so happy to work here. This has to be the best dental practice ever."

"WOW! Where are all these new customers coming from?"

"WOW! Dr. J is awesome. He really listens to my ideas on how to run things more efficiently."

"WOW! Dr. J – thank you!"

Now that I've written these down, I have to see them through. This is the dental practice I have always dreamed of.

Regards,

John

To: Megaphoners
Fm: Sadhana
Re: MegaMagic

PROJECT: GET A MARKETING JOB

Hi everyone,

Just doing this step gave me greater self-confidence and a belief that I can and will get my marketing job. My target was the key marketing managers. Here's the MegaMagic I want after my first round of interviewing with them:

"WOW! Sadhana is serious and has a solid plan to get into marketing. I know there is a place for her."

"WOW! I'm impressed with Sadhana's perseverance. I want to help her out as much as I can."

"WOW! Her insight into marketing is fresh and valuable. I've got to create a job for her."

"WOW! This company is fortunate to have an employee like Sadhana!"

Thinking "WOW!" has changed my perspective on a lot of things. I am more confident and I don't feel as burnt out as I did when I started this an hour or so ago.

Thanks for all your support,

Sadhana

YOUR TURN

What is the MegaMagic for your project?

Remember, you are a Megaphoner ant. You are now crawling around your MegaTarget's conference room. What is it you really want your MegaTarget to say or believe about the MegaBenefits of your project?

When listing your MegaMagic comments from your Mega-Target, remember your Magic Megaphone Principles.

Time to brainstorm . . . and have some fun. Start listing the desired MegaMagic comments with a "WOW!" at the beginning of each sentence. Then transcribe those ideas to your Megaphone tear-out template to complete Step 4.

"WOW! _____ "

"WOW! _____ "

"WOW! _____ "

"WOW! _____ "

SUMMARY OF KEY MEGAMAGIC POINTS:

- Think "WOW!" Why settle for less?
- Be bold, idealistic. Don't be a wimp
- Do not be influenced by past disappointments
- Listen like an ant in your MegaTarget's office
- Use motivational words
- MegaMagic comments are tied to your MegaTarget

MAGIC MEGAPHONE in progress. Here is how Phyllis's Magic Megaphone looks after identifying her MegaMagic:

PHYLLIS

PROJECT: FINANCE EMPLOYEE RECOGNITION TASK FORCE

MegaMission™	MegaBenefits™	MegaPlan™	MegaMagic™	MegaTargets™
			"Wow! That was awesome. My work is really valued and appreciated here."	All Finance employees
			"Wow! I am really glad to be a part of this organization. Thank you."	CFO
	Employee satisfaction			HR manager that supports Finance
	Link performance to group objectives		"Wow! The recognition team did an outstanding job. The best recognition system I have experienced."	Bob (Finance Mgr. sponsoring this project)
	Fosters great workplace value			Judy P. (On Finance staff - key influencer)
Recognize employees for a job well done	Provides consistency with other departments		"Wow! Finance is a great place to work."	Country Managers: SH, TE and GG
	Engagement and retention of employees		"Wow! This means so much to me. I really worked hard on this task and I wasn't sure that management even noticed. Now, I know they do."	Tanya (Admin team lead and key partner)
	. . .			Barry (my manager and peer to Bob)

Make sure the MegaMagic portion of your Magic Megaphone is filled out in a similar fashion.

A final note on Step 4: We all want to hear the sounds of MegaMagic from our MegaTargets. It is one thing to construct such a dream list. But it is another thing to make it all happen.

You must have a plan. That's Step 5.

MegaPlan

getting

into

action

IN STEP 4, YOU LISTED ALL THE PRAISES you want to hear from your MegaTarget. Did you notice how your project team came alive making their MegaMagic list? Now let's turn that MegaMagic into reality.

Nothing will happen or change without action. Step 5 helps your project team identify the actions and changes you must execute to get unstuck and set your project back on the path to success. We call it your MegaPlan.™

Ask your project team to think quickly and boldly – *brainstorm* – and list the actions that are likely to prompt the MegaMagic praises you seek from your MegaTarget. Get everyone involved. Ideas must flow freely.

ASK THESE QUESTIONS OF YOUR TEAM

WHAT ACTIONS MUST we take to make the MegaMagic a reality for our MegaTarget?

How WILL our MegaTarget experience (see, hear, read) our MegaBenefits?

77

YOU ARE LIKELY to list many possible actions. Do not worry if the list becomes long. In brainstorming, all ideas count.

Also, do not worry whether the list is 100% complete. *It will never be complete.* You do not have the resources and time to do everything, so just aim for 85% completeness.

Once the brainstorming has run its course, it is time to make choices.

ASK — Ask your team to rank the list.

VOTE — Vote on *the top three to five actions or tactics* that will have the most influence and impact *given scant time and resources.*

CHOOSE — Choose the three most productive Mega-Plan tactics and execute them well. Your MegaTarget should react just as you want them to – that is the MegaMagic of it all.

EXPECT — Expect MegaMagic results!

Remember the Magic Megaphone Principles as you brainstorm the MegaPlan. Keep it simple. Think bullet points, not sentences.

SYNC UP TIME

We now check in with your fellow Magic Megaphoners to see how they are doing with their MegaPlans.

Magic Megaphone
Principles

1. SIMPLE IS BETTER
2. 85% IS OK
3. THINK "WOW!"

Project: IT Manufacturing Engineering Consolidation

Here's the question I asked the team:

What needs to happen for our MegaTarget to say that we exceeded expectations; that the MegaTarget is receiving great feedback from our manufacturing partners; and that this initiative is a great example of IT adding value?

I was surprised at the team's innovative ideas. We had so many that we had to vote on our top eight and then we dwindled that down to four. The four are circled.

1. Get at least one manufacturing partner on the team.

2. Develop presentation material outlining the new organization's vision, mission and plans.

3. Conduct a road show for employees highlighting the benefits of consolidation.

4. Engage our internal marketing organization to develop a marketing and communication plan.

5. Define our consolidated indicators and goals.

6. Get our new web site up and running immediately.

7. Brief every manager and supervisor on expectations and get them excited about what we are doing.

8. Benchmark against other companies.

PROJECT: IT MANUFACTURING ENGINEERING CONSOLIDATION

We thought all eight were important and needed to be done, but we picked our top four based on what needed to be accomplished first. We assigned 'owners' to each of the four – actually, they volunteered. It was great! The owners then committed to a date and we agreed to a weekly review of our MegaPlan.

A team member commented that we might eventually have gotten to this point, but it was unheard of to get to this stage *in less than an hour.* Everyone agreed that we need to do a Magic Megaphone at the start of every project, and not wait till we are stalled and stuck.

Later,

Carlos

To: Megaphoners

Fm: Phyllis

Re: MegaPlan

Page 1 of 2

PROJECT: FINANCE EMPLOYEE RECOGNITION TASK FORCE

I appreciated getting the e-mail from Carlos before I started Step 5, because it gave me a good idea of how to ask the question to my team. I picked one of the MegaMagic statements that I thought summarized what we were really after. I asked:

What do we need to do for our finance employees to believe that we have the best recognition system they have ever experienced?

Like Carlos, we came up with a really good plan. We had a lot of awesome input to choose from. Here's our list. The circles are the ones we decided to work on immediately.

1. Survey Finance employees.

2. The supply chain organization has a good recognition system. Let's learn from them.

3. All Finance managers need to agree. So, we need a Finance manager plan.

4. Make the employee recognition program easy to administer. Put it on-line.

5. We need to meet weekly instead of monthly.

6. Send out a weekly progress report to all Finance managers.

7. Develop training for all managers and supervisors on how best to recognize employees.

8. Develop a prototype recognition system within two weeks.

To: MEGAPHONERS
FM: PHYLLIS
RE: MEGAPLAN
PAGE 2 OF 2

PROJECT: FINANCE EMPLOYEE RECOGNITION TASK FORCE

9. Define key milestones and deliverables.

10. Develop a follow-up process with recognized employees to make sure we're hitting the mark.

Team members readily volunteered to 'own' the key action items. I would never have imagined we could get this far this fast. We have a plan – yeah!

Bye for now,

Phyllis

To: MEGAPHONERS
FM: JOHN
RE: MEGAPLAN

PROJECT: GROW DENTAL PRACTICE

Here's the plan:

1. Hire a qualified financial planner.
2. Develop a five-year business plan.
3. Define and execute on a training plan for the staff.
4. Improve the scheduling process.
5. Develop an incentive program for staff members.
6. Improve patient/insurance payment processes.
7. Hire an associate.
8. Have the hygiene staff develop a plan for hygiene business growth.
9. Personal energy plan; get serious about fitness and nutrition.

I cannot tackle this entirely on my own. I do know of a dental practice consultant I can hire who can help me with several of the items. She comes highly recommended. Also, I need to engage my staff as soon as possible and have them be responsible for a few of these. The others – as Nike's slogan goes, "Just Do It." And, I will.

John

To: Megaphoners
Fm: Sadhana
Re: MegaPlan

Project: Get a Marketing Job

I took a bold step. I knew that a key action would be to obtain a marketing mentor, so I asked one of the key marketing managers, JB, for a one on one meeting. He agreed to be my mentor. In that meeting I shared my Magic Megaphone and asked for his help in completing the MegaPlan. He was so impressed, he said, "I can tell you really want this and I know you'll do great. I will help you out as much as I can." I could not believe it. Those words are almost verbatim in my MegaMagic.

He made a few phone calls and has already set me up to meet a few managers who have entry-level marketing positions open. He also asked me to share the Magic Megaphone process with his staff. He thought his entire team could really put it to good use. Wow!

Here is the MegaPlan JB helped me create:

1. Take all available marketing classes the company offers.

2. Take advantage of the mentor program – DONE.

3. Meet with a career and education counselor and determine an education plan. The company provides this service.

4. Talk to my current boss and gain his support.

5. Update my resumé and be sure to include the engineering jobs in which I dealt directly with customers.

6. Establish relationships with the other two key marketing managers through one-on-one meetings.

I am trying to avoid getting my hopes up too high; however, I can't help it. It's almost scary how fast this Magic Megaphone is working. For the first time in a long time, I am excited about working for this company.

Sadhana

YOUR TURN to define your MegaPlan

If you have not already done so, list those key actions that need to be taken before your MegaTarget is likely to utter those MegaMagic praises.

1. _____

2. _____

3. _____

4. _____

5. _____

6. _____

7. _____

8. _____

9. _____

10. _____

11. _____

12. _____

Good job.

Now select the top three to five actions that need immediate attention. Have various team members take responsibility for specific actions.

Remember to transfer this to your own Magic Megaphone tear-out template.

MEASURING the progress of your Magic Megaphone

Four simple MegaPlan tracking points are all that are needed for you and your team members to manage the MegaPlan and measure accountability:

- What SPECIFIC AUDIENCE is your target for a particular action?
- WHAT is the specific action or change to be implemented?
- WHICH TEAM MEMBER must take responsibility or *ownership* for that action to make it happen?
- What is the DUE DATE for completing that action?

SUMMARY OF KEY MEGAPLAN POINTS

- Pose a question to start the brainstorming
- Select the top three to five as your next steps
- Simple is better
- 85% is OK
- Identify an owner for each selected action
- Ensure each team member commits to a completion date for each assigned action item

After an hour's work, here are the completed Magic Megaphones and MegaPlans from Carlos, Phyllis, John, and Sadhana.

CARLOS

PROJECT: IT MANUFACTURING ENGINEERING CONSOLIDATION

MEGAMISSION™	MEGABENEFITS™	MEGAPLAN™	MEGAMAGIC™	MEGATARGETS™
Best mfg computing support organization in the world	Increase volume and reduce TPT (throughput time) Sets up manufacturing as a competitive advantage Enables IT to be proactive vs. reactive Quality increase Reduces TCO Increases IT value to the company ...	1. Get at least one mfg partner on the team 2. Develop an entire consolidation package for our upcoming mgt meeting that includes the new organization's vision, mission, and plans 3. Conduct a road show for our employees and our mfg partners highlighting the benefits of consolidation 4. Engage our internal marketing organization to help us with a marketing and communication plan 5. Define our consolidated indicators and goals 6. Get our new web site up and running ASAP 7. Train every manager and supervisor in our org on expectations 8. Benchmark against other companies	"Wow! This team not only executed flawlessly on the consolidation plan, but they provided a vision the entire organization can get behind" "Wow! I'm inspired. The team deserves our full support" "Wow! This is a fine example of how IT really adds value to our company" "Wow! Our manufacturing partners are already experiencing the benefit of the consolidation. I'm getting tons of positive feedback" "Wow! This team demonstrated leadership and exceeded my expectations"	Manufacturing management team: Bob, GW, EH Tan, Pat, Jason CIO and her direct staff Michael (our boss) All IT Manufacturing employees (consolidated team) to help All Manufacturing employees (users) IT Manufacturing Engineering mgt. team

CARLOS

MEGAPLAN			
MEGATARGET	ACTION	OWNER	DUE DATE
IT Mfg Engineering mgt team	Get at least one manufacturing partner representative on our project team.	CD	1 week
	Develop an entire consolidation package for our upcoming mgt meeting that includes presentation material and video outlining the new organization's vision, mission and plans.	Carlos	2 weeks
	Develop our marketing and communication plan.	TG	1 week
	Define our consolidated indicators and goals.	JA	1 week

Ant Wisdom

"If our original plan had had a lower goal, we would have achieved less."

William Foster, CEO, Stratus

PHYLLIS

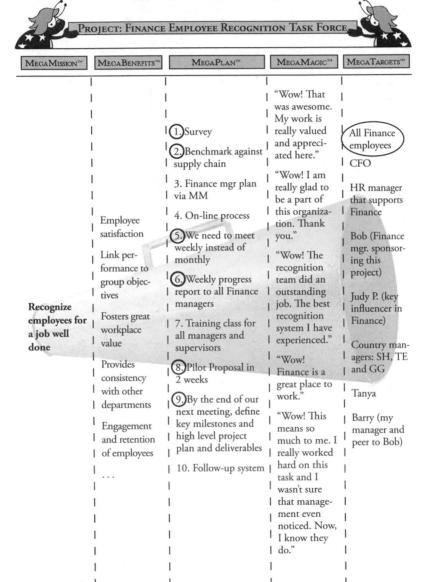

PROJECT: FINANCE EMPLOYEE RECOGNITION TASK FORCE

MegaMission™	MegaBenefits™	MegaPlan™	MegaMagic™	MegaTargets™
Recognize employees for a job well done	Employee satisfaction Link performance to group objectives Fosters great workplace value Provides consistency with other departments Engagement and retention of employees ...	1. Survey 2. Benchmark against supply chain 3. Finance mgr plan via MM 4. On-line process 5. We need to meet weekly instead of monthly 6. Weekly progress report to all Finance managers 7. Training class for all managers and supervisors 8. Pilot Proposal in 2 weeks 9. By the end of our next meeting, define key milestones and high level project plan and deliverables 10. Follow-up system	"Wow! That was awesome. My work is really valued and appreciated here." "Wow! I am really glad to be a part of this organization. Thank you." "Wow! The recognition team did an outstanding job. The best recognition system I have experienced." "Wow! Finance is a great place to work." "Wow! This means so much to me. I really worked hard on this task and I wasn't sure that management even noticed. Now, I know they do."	All Finance employees CFO HR manager that supports Finance Bob (Finance mgr. sponsoring this project) Judy P. (key influencer in Finance) Country managers: SH, TE and GG Tanya Barry (my manager and peer to Bob)

PHYLLIS

MEGAPLAN			
MEGATARGET	ACTION	OWNER	DUE DATE
All Finance employees	Send out a quick survey to Finance employees and learn from them what they think makes an outstanding recognition system.	HD	1 week
	The supply chain organization is well regarded as having a good recognition system. Let's go talk to them and understand what works and what doesn't work.	SS	1 week
	We need to meet weekly instead of monthly.	ALL	DONE
	Send out a weekly progress report to all Finance managers.	Phyllis	Weekly
	We need a starting point. Within two weeks, come in with a proposal for a recognition system.	TM	2 weeks
	By the end of our next meeting, define key milestones and high level project plan and deliverables.	Phyllis	1 week

Ant Wisdom

"How many things are looked upon as quite impossible until they have been actually effected."

Pliny the Elder

JOHN

PROJECT: GROW DENTAL PRACTICE

MegaMission™	MegaBenefits™	MegaPlan™	MegaMagic™	MegaTargets™
		1. Hire a qualified financial planner	"WOW! There's a business plan for growth, and I'm part of it."	
		2. Develop a 5 year business plan	"WOW! Dr. J is on it. There is definitely renewed energy and exitement in the office. I'm going to be on it, too."	My family
	Financial security	3. Define and execute on a training plan for the staff		My staff
		4. Improve the scheduling process		Current patients
	No-worry college funding	5. Develop an incentive program for staff members	"WOW! I am so happy to work here. This has to be the best dentist practice ever."	New patients
50 in 3	Greater disposable income	6. Improve patient/insurance payment processes		My vendors
	More efficiency		"WOW! Where are all these new customer coming from?"	Community organizations I volunteer at
	Growth opportunites for employees	7. Hire an associate		My dental association
	More opportunites to give back to the community	8. Have the hygiene staff develop a plan for hygiene staff business growth	"WOW! Dr. J is awesome. He really listens to my ideas on how to run things more efficiently."	
	. . .	9. Personal energy plan; get serious about fitness and nutrition	"WOW! Dr. J – thank you!"	

JOHN

MEGAPLAN			
MEGATARGET	ACTION	OWNER	DUE DATE
My staff	Hire a qualified financial planner.	John	3 wks
	Develope a 5-year business plan.	John & FP	8 wks
	Define and execute on a training plan for the staff.	John & consultant	12 wks
	Improve the scheduling process.	Staff & consultant	16 wks
	Develop an incentive program for staff members.	John & consultant	16 wks
	Hire an associate.	John & consultant	16 wks
	Have the hygiene staff develop a plan for hygiene business growth.	Staff & consultant	8 wks
	Personal energy plan; get serious about fitness and nutrition.	John	NOW!

Ant Wisdom

"Our plans miscarry because they have no aim. When a man does not know what harbor he is making for, no wind is the right wind."

Seneca

SADHANA

PROJECT: GET A MARKETING JOB

MegaMission™	MegaBenefits™	MegaPlan™	MegaMagic™	MegaTargets™
Get a marketing job	Company retains a good employee Match passion with job Utilize software engineering experience in marketing realm Less stress Increased productivity . . .	①. Take all available marketing classes the company offers ②. Take advantage of the mentor program – DONE ③. Meet with a career and education counselor and determine an education plan. The company provides this service ④. Talk to my current boss and gain his support ⑤. Update my resume and be sure to include the engineering jobs in which I dealt directly with customers ⑥. Establish relationships with the other two key marketing managers through one on one meetings. Include TL	"WOW! Sadhana is serious and has a solid plan to get into marketing. I know there is a place for her." "WOW! I'm impressed with Sadhana's perseverence. I want to help her as much as I can." "WOW! Her insight into marketing is fresh and valuable. I've got to create a job for her." "WOW! This company is fortunate to have an employee like Sadhana."	Phillip (my current boss) Kristen (my HR rep) RL, AM and JB (key marketing managers) Rav (my fiancé) My family (Mother & Father) John W. (my boss's boss) Faye (a friend of mine in marketing who is highly regarded and influential)

SADHANA

MEGAPLAN			
MEGATARGET	ACTION	OWNER	DUE DATE
RL, AM & JB	Take all available marketing classes the company offers.	Sadhana	Sign up in 2 wks
	Take advantage of the mentor program.	Sadhana	DONE
	Meet with a career and education counselor and determine an educational plan. The company provides this service.	Sadhana	4 weeks
	Talk to my current boss and gain his support.	Sadhana	Next 2 days
	Update my resume and be sure to include the engineering jobs in which I dealt directly with customers.	Sadhana	1 week
	Establish relationships with the other two key marketing managers through one-on-one meetings.	Sadhana	3 wks

Ant Wisdom

*"Make no little plans:
they have no magic to stir men's blood."*

The Motto of the City Planner
by Daniel Burnham

GRADUATION

CONGRATULATIONS! You are now an official Megaphoner.

- You now have a completed Magic Megaphone and a plan of action.

- All team members are now working from the same plan. That plan is easy to follow and easy to measure because it is only two pages long. (No huge binders needed here.)

Display your Magic Megaphone as a daily reminder on your desk, bulletin board, or as a screen saver.

STAYING UNSTUCK & MONITORING RESULTS

To stay unstuck, you need to follow-up. Ask your project team, perhaps weekly, to monitor how the MegaPlan is working and how team members are doing with their assigned action items. Many teams include Magic Megaphone check-ins as part of their regular project meeting process.

What about the other MegaPlan actions that did not make it to the top of the list? What about the other MegaTargets that were not selected? The check-in monitors such questions as:

- Are we done with MegaTarget A?

- Can we go on to MegaTarget B?

- Are we ready for the next MegaPlan item?

Give yourself a few weeks to make significant progress on your newly created Magic Megaphone. After that, you have some options: Select additional MegaPlan actions to work on, or select another MegaTarget and develop a MegaPlan for that new target.

A MegaPlan can change to fit a specific target audience – or individual. But you will likely find that once you select the main target, much of what you do for that MegaTarget will apply to the others on your original MegaTarget list.

Your project's MegaMission and MegaBenefits will likely not change. They are the foundation to your project.

Now, for one last check-in with your fellow Megaphoners.

SIX WEEKS LATER . . . .

To: Megaphoners
Fm: Carlos
Re: Six weeks later

Project: IT Manufacturing Engineering Consolidation

So much has happened during the last six weeks, I don't know where to begin. Three weeks ago, we presented the plan to our management team (our MegaTarget) and their reaction was awesome. The best decision we made was to include a manufacturing partner on our team. Ron's contribution kept us focused.

The project team continues to be highly motivated and we've developed our second megaphone – this one aimed at *all IT mfg employees*. Once we gained management support, we refocused to gain the support of our entire organization.

My manager told me that I have exceeded his expectations and have demonstrated a higher level of leadership. (Again, more MegaMagic).

I have also been asked by our manufacturing partners to share the Magic Megaphone process with their teams. This has helped establish stronger relationships with them.

I wish you the best of luck in your projects.

Carlos

To: Megaphoners
Fm: Phyllis
Re: Six weeks later

PROJECT: FINANCE EMPLOYEE RECOGNITION TASK FORCE

Hi everyone,

It's been one "magic" ride. As it turned out, our initial action plan was right on. Understanding other departments' systems and getting employee feedback really paid off. We just completed some pilots and employees loved the process. Believe it or not, we heard MegaMagic comments time and again from the employees who participated. We are implementing the full program in two weeks time. I'm confident it will go well.

I remember my first comments to you and how stuck I felt. It's hard to believe that was only a few weeks ago. I find myself using the Magic Megaphone tool for all projects, both in and out of work. My family now calls me Mama Megaphone.

Keep the magic,

Phyllis

To: Megaphoners
Fm: John
Re: Six weeks later

PROJECT: GROW DENTAL PRACTICE

Sadhana, Phyllis and Carlos,

Just yesterday, I made an offer on a new building to accommodate the expansion of my practice. That highly recommended consultant is on board and the staff is working well with her in identifying areas for efficiency and training.

The energy in the office is at its highest level ever. Even patients are commenting positively about the change in the environment and attitude from the staff. Financial planning is well underway and the new building is part of the growth plan. I've begun the search for an associate and there are several qualified candidates.

My personal energy is up. I joined a gym and I work out four times per week.

I hope all is well with each of you. As we were learning the Magic Megaphone process, your insights were invaluable to me and, for that, I will forever be grateful.

John

To: Megaphoners
Fm: Sadhana
Re: Six weeks later

Project: Get a Marketing Job

Hello fellow Megaphoners,

It's good to write to you once again. I am faced with a tough decision. I now have two job offers in marketing and one of them is an external offer. After writing my resumé, I sent it to a few other companies and I heard back from all of them. Also, JB has worked hard to put me in touch with the right people and I now have an offer from one of them for an entry level marketing position. The external position offers a higher salary, but will not pay for continuing education. I'm leaning towards accepting the internal offer so that I can obtain a degree in business/marketing. This is a good problem to have. It's great to know that the Megaphone worked its magic.

Thank you for helping me get unstuck. I have a new lease on life.

My fondest regards,

Sadhana

Part Two

MegaSuccesses

More examples of how

The Magic Megaphone

works in *any* organization

MegaSuccesses

four more

success stories

based upon actual projects

YOU HAVE COMPLETED YOUR MAGIC Megaphone along with Carlos, Phyllis, John, and Sadhana. You are now unstuck.

MORE MEGASUCCESSES

If you want to see more case studies of the Magic Megaphone in action, we have included four more success stories based on actual projects. Only names have been changed or omitted in accordance with company proprietary guidelines.

We want to hear of your Magic Megaphone successes. Look us up on www.magicmegaphone.com and submit your MegaSuccess story. You can also learn of how others are successfully applying their Magic Mcgaphones.

MegaSuccess #1

IT staff
enlightens company's
sales conference

EACH YEAR THE COMPANY'S INFORMATION Technology (IT) group is involved with the annual sales and marketing conference. IT's involvement had been solely to set up a technical assistance center that provides computer support for conference attendees.

In 2003, Josh headed the IT support team for the conference. He and his fellow IT leaders had an idea. They were convinced that IT expertise could help the sales force because many of their customers were IT organizations.

Josh's team was asked to increase IT support and visibility at the sales conference and thereby show company executives that their own internal IT group could play a major role in product sales.

In 2003, wireless was a reality and wireless support would be expected. But how would IT execute it? With only two months to prepare, time was running out. Josh and his team were stuck and needed help!

Josh asked Nick Montoya for assistance. Nick told him to assemble his team the next day for a Magic Megaphone session. The team finished the Magic Megaphone in less than 60 minutes, leaving them with a clear vision and plan for exceeding their leaders' expectations.

PROJECT: IT AT SALES CONFERENCE

MegaMission™	MegaBenefits™	MegaPlan™	MegaMagic™	MegaTargets™
			"Wow! IT really showed what mobility is all about."	
	Biz improves			
	Minimized impact of being away for a week	1. Signage & common theme	"Wow! IT team – so awesome – we need to partner with them."	
	Knowledge/ info sharing re: selling to IT	2. Uniformity		CEO
		③ Wireless – experience the future now	"Wow! We haven't fully utilized our IT expertise – let's do it."	VP Mktg & staff
	Mkt/sell base technologies	④ CIO keynote		VP Sales & Staff
		⑤ IT classes by IT senior professionals		Business development managers
Help company market & sell	Mobility promise in action		"Wow! We can't succeed w/o IT."	
	Showcase	6. Solution Booth		Sales force attendees
	Provide solutions	⑦ Help Desk	"Wow! Great Technology."	
		8. Cyber Café	"Wow! IT is so cool. I want to work there!"	
	Be able to talk w/authority & experience to customers	⑨ Train IT staff for conference	"Wow! I'm a believer ... IT is truly the ACE in the Hole!"	
	...	⑩ Field tools	"Wow! What great collaboration tools."	

J osh's group was relieved to be unstuck. "The Megaphone guided us in our sales conference project and in our goal of using our experience and expertise to help Intel sales educate customers' IT shops."

"Like magic, the executives we selected as our MegaTargets said the MegaMagic almost verbatim. Our performance at this conference paved the way for the IT partnership program and, more importantly, proved to our IT folks that we could add greater value to company operations."

"During the Megaphone session, everyone's creativity was sparked. We developed a theme for IT's involvement that we called 'Experience The Future Now.' It was the rallying point for more than 100 IT people working on the project."

MegaSuccess #2

The
Del Campo
Dance Studio

MIKE DEL CAMPO AND HIS WIFE GINA
own Del Campo Dance Studio where they teach primarily
Latin dancing.

Like so many small business owners, Mike started his business around a passion and skill: dance instruction. Many people who try to turn their passion and skill into a business fail because they don't have the business savvy or background to sustain long-term success.

Author Nick Montoya's daughter was taking classes at Del Campo. "I could see the quality of the dance instruction was high, but running the business seemed to be a lower priority," Nick observed. "I offered Mike a trade. I would facilitate a Magic Megaphone for his business in return for some dance lessons for my daughter." Mike agreed.

Here's the Magic Megaphone that resulted after spending one hour with Mike and Gina:

PROJECT: DEL CAMPO DANCE STUDIO

MegaMission™	MegaBenefits™	MegaPlan™	MegaMagic™	MegaTargets™
Make Del Campo the #1 Latin dance studio in Sacramento	More students, means more revenue to: - Pay for expansion - Keep good instructors - Invest in dance teams - Loyal instructor and student base - Introduce Latin dancing to a wider audience - Healthy activity for all ages and for families - Having a good reputation yields corporate sponsorships . . .	1. Develop mailing list and contact info of all students, past and present 2. Up-level business website 3. Tracking process for all people attending group lessons 4. Develop an incentive plan for students 5. Add at least one additional dance troupe 6. Develop a training plan for instructors on how best to recruit and teach in order to obtain long-term student retention	"Wow! this is fun and I'm learning a lot." "Wow! I've got to bring my friends and family." "Wow! I feel as if though I belong to the Del Campo Family. They make me feel right at home!" "Wow! the dance instruction here is the best!"	Current instructors Current students Salsa Capital Dance Troupe Festival organizers Sacramento Hispanic Chamber of Commerce All persons interested in Latin dancing in Sacramento region Past students

Mike Del Campo was relieved to have a plan: "At first, I was skeptical about the process, even though I knew I needed some business focus. However, I didn't want to pay thousands of dollars for a business consultant."

"In less than an hour, Nick helped me get focused on a few key items that made a tremendous, positive impact on my business. It was simple and easy to understand. The process helped me get my dance instruction team on the same page."

"I'm happy to say that Del Campo Dance Studio is now considered the #1 studio for Latin dancing in the Sacramento region, just as we stated in the MegaMission."

MEGASUCCESS #3

a

mom

on a mission

KAREN WAS THE PRESIDENT OF A COMPANY'S internal Parents' Network, one of several employee groups that focus on various issues or concerns. Her biggest challenge was to educate managers. Many managers are not parents and thus are not aware of the circumstances parents face that can affect job performance.

Karen performed this extracurricular role in addition to her regular job. But she was spending too much time on it, and her manager was hinting she reduce the time spent. What's more, Karen's Parents' Network leadership team had not been successful in engaging member parents to take a more active role.

Karen was stuck! She asked Nick Montoya to facilitate a Magic Megaphone for her leadership team.

The first question asked was, "Why does the Parents' Network exist?" The immediate response was, "To be successful employees and parents." To do this, we needed to reach parent employees.

Their mission statement was:

To support parents in our workplace in an attempt to balance more effectively work and life in hopes of achieving higher productivity for the company and happier employees.

The team quickly saw the need for a brief, obvious statement that would stick with parent members. They needed a simple MegaMission.

PROJECT: PARENTS' NETWORK

MegaMission™	MegaBenefits™	MegaPlan™	MegaMagic™	MegaTargets™
Be a successful parent *and* employee.	Healthy, happy employees Productivity increase Networking & sharing opportunities Build confidence as parent & employee Educational Influence company re: parental issues Leadership & visibility opportunities for members . . .	1. Obtain a visible and key senior manager as a sponsor for PN 2. Implement a compelling speaker series for members 3. Insure managers of PN members acknowledge and recognize involvement 4. Understand the top issues preventing involvement from current members via survey or focus group 5. Provide testimonials on the value and benefit of PN 6. Recruit motivated individuals to fulfill leadership roles 7. Develop an intranet site for up-to-date information on PN activities	"Wow! I am part of a great community here at this company." "Wow! I've enhanced my parenting skills through participation with PN." "Wow! I've decided to stay at this company because of the great support for parents. It's a great place to work!" "Wow! I feel valued as a parent." "Wow! My manager supports and encourages my involvement with PN."	All employees who are parents Current parent network members Key managers in HR: C.A., M.T., B.E.; Employees considering parenthood; Company senior managers and site committees

Parents' Network is now regarded as one of the top employee groups in the company. "We have exceeded all our membership and activity goals."

"We have recruited an awesome leadership team. The team members are not afraid of doing their share of the work. I am now able to effectively balance my time with my regular job and I have even benefited in terms of being a better parent."

MegaSuccess #4

special
products division
needed a comeback

THE SPECIAL PRODUCTS DIVISION (SPD) of a large corporation was trying to recover from the cancellation of two major projects and the resulting reorganization and potential lay-offs. The tremendous changes drove morale to the depths. SPD's senior management team felt stuck on how to re-energize employees.

The Magic Megaphone process was still in its infancy within the Division. SPD leaders heard about the unique sessions and asked Nick Montoya to facilitate one for them. Here is the Magic Megaphone they developed.

| | | PROJECT: RESTORING DIVISION MORALE | | | |

MegaMission™	MegaBenefits™	MegaPlan™	MegaMagic™	MegaTargets™
Create business opportunities that extend company return on assets (ROA)	A renewed confidence in leadership Profitable division Continued employment Exercises creativity, flexibility, and risk-taking Customer orientation is a must Requires partnership with company's mainstream products …	① Do Megaphones at the team level ② Communicate, communicate, communicate… ③ SPD Team Day ④ Recognize, recognize, recognize… ⑤ Profitability events and celebrations ⑥ Ensure 1:1's are happening ⑦ Learning organization	"Wow! What a comeback, and I was a key part of it!" "Wow! We have a future and our future is bright." "Wow! We truly are a learning organization." "Wow! 'No Limits' is real." "Wow! Breakthroughs are a way of life for us."	Our employees

SPD was able to recover quickly, regain profitability, and avoid any lay-offs.

As one SPD leader said, "I saw the successes Nick was having with other teams using this simple Magic Megaphone concept and asked him to help us. After conducting the session for the management team, Nick was in high demand and probably conducted more than fifty Megaphones for the remainder of the year."

"I can't say that is was the Megaphone itself that turned this division around. But I can say that it was the catalyst for positive change. It helped enroll our employees in articulating what success would look like."

MegaQuestions

typical
questions you
may be asked

NOW THAT YOU ARE AN OFFICIAL Mega-
phoner, you are likely to be asked many questions about the
Magic Megaphone.

Here are some typical questions and answers to help you:

Q: Hey, we've got a business to run here. All this stuff about
mega this and mega that. Come on. There's no substance
here...too simplified. How can it work here?

A: *It's a proven method. It's worked at companies large and
small. It worked in the book's eight case stories.*

*How would you rate your projects? How fast do teams come
together? Are your teams ready in 60 minutes . . . or days?*

*We understand detailed analysis has its place. But you can't ana-
lyze much if you are stuck dead in the mud. This process is about
getting unstuck and up and running.*

Q: This thing about 85% completeness . . . that isn't going to go over well here. We need 100% success or our competitors will roll over us.

A: *Here's our point in a nutshell: If you identify only 85% of the possibilities – and actually tackle and solve them – the remaining 15% may well fall into place without any further action. But striving for 100% perfection delays getting started. What's more, once you accomplish the 85%, you can go on to tackle the remaining 15% if they haven't already been solved.*

Q: This "WOW!" thing . . . very idealistic, don't you think? We don't live in a perfect world, and many of our execs are just not that warm and fuzzy. What's more, your 85% thing seems to contradict your idealistic wow thing. What's that about?

A: *It isn't contradictory. If your project quickly accomplishes the top 85% of the possibilities, you are adding real value. We want to enliven project teams with big goals. That whole MegaMagic section makes participants come alive because they are so used to mediocre results. End that nonsense! Try liberating a team for a change. When you were in school, weren't you enlivened by A+ grades? So aim for them in your projects, too.*

To make sure your Magic Megaphone delivers for you:

- Don't impose a Megaphone on a team. Allow the team members to develop it.

- Don't force a long mission statement on the project. Instead, aim for a quick and easy MegaMission. One sentence.

- Don't be overly general about MegaTargets. Be specific. It may be one individual who controls your project's destiny.

- Aim for the 85% completeness you can execute.

- Regularly check-in on your MegaPlan to measure progress.

"WOW!"

We could not have done it
without you!

Cathy   Giana   Elisa
Lia   Jason   J. Anita
Rachel   Dan   Jeanne
Joe   Sophie   Diana
Mark   Janiece
Glen   Carlos
Chris   JJ
Karen   Sanjay
Mike   Gina
Craig   John W.
Josh   Cleon
Barb   John S.
Bob   Vicki
Alice   Monica
Julie   Phyllis
Judy

Nick and Roger

| MegaMission™ | MegaBenefits™ | MegaPlan™ | MegaMagic™ | MegaTargets™ |

MegaPlan

MEGATARGET	ACTION	OWNER	DUE DATE

PROJECT: _____

| MEGAMISSION™ | MEGABENEFITS™ | MEGAPLAN™ | MEGAMAGIC™ | MEGATARGETS™ |

MegaPlan

MEGATARGET	ACTION	OWNER	DUE DATE

PROJECT: _____

| MegaMission™ | MegaBenefits™ | MegaPlan™ | MegaMagic™ | MegaTargets™ |

MegaPlan

MEGATARGET	ACTION	OWNER	DUE DATE